Mr & Mrs Mouse

~and their~

MAGICAL ALPHABET HOUSE

Kate Toms

make believe ideas

Mr and Mrs Mouse

were a pair of highly unusual mice.
They had a collection of curious things
such as dominoes, donkeys and dice!

But their house was so full that all of their things
would get lost in the piles on the floor.
"We need a plan!" exclaimed Mrs Mouse,
"Our house just can't hold any more!"

Just at that moment, the door opened wide
and the alphabet wizard stepped in!
"I think I can help you to clear up your house!"
the wizard exclaimed with a grin.

He waved his wand, and the house was transformed –
now it had twelve giant rooms!
The first had a sign that declared "A and B"
and was piled high with apples and brooms.

The next room was crowded with things that began
with either a C or a D.
But the mice didn't know if their things were all there –
there were so many objects to see!

So Mr and Mrs Mouse need your help
to sort out the rooms a bit better.
Can you find the objects around every page,
and make sure they start with that letter?

bird • boat • blackboard

ball •

bears •

bus

 butterfly • ballerina • basket

dice • doll • dominoes

dog

drum

duck

  dinosaur • donkey • door

egg

eyes

emerald eyes

•  giraffe

 • grapes

 • goat

  game • 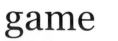 goldfish •  goose

hat • harmonica • hedgehog

 H

hammer • heart • horn

 horse •  Humpty Dumpty • house

 ivy

 igloo

 icing

knot

kangaroo

kiwi

lion • lighthouse • ladder

lollipops • lock • lemon

 lace •  leaf • letter

mirror

milk

music

nail •

numbers •

nuts

oranges •  owl • peanuts

 octopus • oil •  pineapple

P

 penguin • pear •  plate

 pumpkin •

 pencil •

 pie

 paints • pine cone •  pig

 P

 quiche •  queen • rosette

 strawberry •  spider •  spoon

U  **unicorn** • **up** • **valentine**

 udder •  **umbrella** •  **unicycle**

  upside down • **underwear** •  **violets**

 violin • vacuum cleaner • vase

vegetables • vehicle • vinegar

 vest •  vowels • volcano

windmill •  whisk • weight

 **W**

 whistle

 wool

 wool

 wand

 wand

is for ZOO where the animals live

 Y

 yo-yo •  yolk •  yogurt • yogurt

 X-ray • xylophone • fox

 box

•

zebra

•

zero

  zoo • zigzag • zip